Songs for Her & Odes in Her Honor
An English-French Edition

Paul Verlaine
"The Prince of Poets"

Translated By Richard Robinson

Sunny Lou Publishing Company
Portland, Oregon, USA
http://www.sunnyloupublishing.com

2nd Edition, Revised & Corrected: January 7, 2024
Original Publication Date: February 21, 2021

Translation Copyright © 2021 Richard Robinson.
All rights reserved.

ISBN: 978-1-7354776-7-1

Contents

Foreword 5

Songs for Her 11

Odes in Her Honor 39

Chansons pour Elle (French) 69

Odes en Son Honneur (French) 97

Foreword

Whenever I spend time with professors, modern Areopagites, or simple friends and the topic of conversation turns to Paul Verlaine's poetry, – which I have to admit, does not happen all that often – the first things that come to minds and lips are music and nuance. Music and nuance.

Now, we all know what music means when it comes to poetry: rhythm, meter, rhyme, effectively. But when pressed by my interlocutors to toss specifics into the barathrum of the musical argument I'm making, like plug nickles into an empty violin case, and defend a position that they share, I might say things like "end rhymes particularly, masculine rhymes," or, just to sound literary, I might repeat what Huysmans said about Verlaine's poetry, through his mouthpiece Des Esseintes. Here's what that affected esthete, that thrice-decadent son of the family Floressas des Esseintes has to say about it:[1]

> *Muni de rimes obtenues par des temps de verbes, quelquefois même par de longs adverbes précédés d'un monosyllabe d'où ils tombaient comme du rebord d'une pierre, en une cascade pesante d'eau, son vers, coupé par d'invraisemblables césures, devenait souvent singulièrement abstrus, avec ses ellipses audacieuses et ses étranges incorrections qui n'étaient point cependant sans grâce.[2]*

But these musical attributes of Verlaine's poetry, although exemplary, are not unique to him, and a whole library of other poets' works, in English, French, and other languages, Arabic, Greek, *et cætura*, exists, for thousands of years now, from before the library in

---

[1] From chapter XIV of *À rebours*.

[2] *Furnished with rhymes obtained from verb tenses, sometimes even from long adverbs preceded by a monosyllable from which they fell as if over the edge of a rock, in a heavy cascade of water, his verse, interrupted by improbable caesura, often became unusually abstruse, with its bold ellipses and its strange improprieties that were not at all however graceless.*

Alexandria burned down – with those exact same musical (let's say poetic) characteristics.

Nuance requires more explanation: in the case of Paul Verlaine, it boils down to phrases like "par un beau jour de septembre attiédi," "lasse de vivre, ayant peur de mourir," "une aube affaiblie," "Le ciel si pâle et les arbre si grêles," "Le soir tombait, un soir équivoque d'automne"...[3] where so much is tenuous, evanescent, of a memory or of a dream, of a breath hovering in the mystical air, ready to be snatched up by some predatory animal, to vanish behind the bush, or to come crashing down to earth at the slightest misstep or sound. Of course, Verlaine is concrete in many places – but it is his nuance that captures one's attention in especial and remains fixed in the mind and memory – at once and for many years afterwards. "Il pleure dans mon coeur/Comme il pleut sur la ville," is a phrase that has stuck with me since the first time I read it, and to which I have recurred at various moments in my life, for more than thirty years now.

But taken *together*, music and nuance – it is through his heightened employment simultaneously and regularly of those two attributes, of those two mesmerizing attributes of his often absinthe-like poetry, that Paul Verlaine, the poet, really shines, – brightly, not incandescently, but fluorescently, like the greenish-blue polestar on a winter's night as seen through a thin piece of Philomène's batiste or cambric lingerie. With the music and nuance, simultaneously employed, his poetry stands out in a dark, cold, but velvety northern sky, – leaving most other great poets standing, from Tibullus to Robert Frost, along the periphery or against a wall, merely gleaming, fadingly, with embarrassed grins, and rightly so, as if someone, the Big Bear of criticism, had just pulled their trousers down, or the Little Bear of popular dilettantism, their dickies up.

I remember pitching a translation of these same two books of poetry by Verlaine – *Songs for Her* and *Odes in Her Honor* – to a respectable small press in the states recently that showed some interest in the proposal initially. But when the conversation turned to platin-

---

[3]"on a beautiful temperate day of September," "weary of living, afraid of dying," "a dim dawn," "The sky so pale and the trees so spindly," "The evening fell, an equivocal Autumn evening."

um tacks and translation mechanics, and I said I didn't plan to *make* the poems rhyme (but would happily include end rhymes when and where they worked), the conversation faltered quickly and the project was eventually dropped. I since found another publisher[4] who warmed up to my æsthetic, and both books of poetry, translated into English, have been published.

As if the music – the meter, the rhythm, and the rhyme – of a poem in French could ever be translated into English without sacrificing the author's original intent, his intended signification; unless of course the music *is* the intent, but Paul Verlaine, unlike Marshal MacLuhan, is more than that. As if poetry in translation could ever be anything more than an approximation, or loose imitation. It can be an intimation though. And there are always happy occurrences that no translator worth his crushed nutmeg would leave on the cutting board – if they worked. When meaning and meter, the right word and end rhyme, all line up perfectly, like happy stars, with or without undue fudging, that is a miracle. Miracles happen, like the Star of Bethlehem two thousand some odd years ago did, but not often. And, like lightning, they hardly ever strike or fall in the same place twice (scil. poem, or book of poetry). Syllogistically then, when you read a book of poetry originally written in French, translated into English, and the music (meter, rhythm, *and* end rhyme) are all preserved (translated), you can be fairly sure that *something* was sacrificed; given it wasn't the music or the form, it was likely the diction, and its corollary, across multiple lines: the meaning or signification of the poem.

The nuance is easier than the music to get right in idiomatic English translation, from French, almost always.

So what about the music and nuance in the English translation of Paul Verlaine's *Songs for Her* and *Odes in Her Honor*? That's the thing: there isn't any. Nuance. There's music, plenty of it. But the nuance is simply not there, much. By design of the original author. Think about it. If you were going to write a paean (not paeon) to some woman or man, – your "partner" as we say in the extreme West, because we're all cowboys on the last frontier, right? –

---
[4]Sunny Lou Publishing.

if you were going to write a lyric, an ode, a rondeau, or a blazon, in two or twenty-four poems, and you wanted to get as close to the metal, i.e. the flesh, that palpitating knot of voluptuous nerves and muscle, and the orgasm, as close as you could get (without incurring fines or being thrown into prison) – you too probably, like Verlaine, would choose to speak in blunter, but more down-to-earth terms, like breast, belly, nape, loin.

He didn't set out to be Petrarch in these two books of poetry. And neither Philomène, the tantalizing tart at least twenty years his junior, the "her" in *Odes in Her Honor*; nor Eugénie, his practical and good-hearted if not somewhat ugly and thick-necked bed partner, the "her" in *Songs for Her*, – neither of them, those two muses, are like Laura. You, if a poet, might, like Shakespeare, write an anti-blazon for them. Verlaine, instead, wrote positive blazons, with all the talent he possessed, and little nuance.

Appreciators of Verlaine's poetry who have thus far cast in their critical two-thumbs-up, five-stars, or ten-tomatoes assessment of his verse as based on the first four or six or seven volumes of poetry he wrote – as most readers and appreciators of Verlaine happen to do, from 1896 until now – from *Poèmes saturniens*, assuredly, to *Romances sans paroles*, without a doubt, and possibly later, to *Cellulairement, Sagesse* or *Jadis et Naguère* even (the best lyrical pieces of which were written while incarcerated in Mons Prison, and some of those from events, recollected in tranquil captivity, that happened earlier in time, in the period during or just following *Romances sans paroles*) – will be disappointed. At first blush. When reading *Songs for Her* or *Odes in Her Honor*. Because of misplaced and misguided expectations. But if one leaves one's expectations, along with one's hat, at the door, the indulgent reader may find that the informal, popular songs found in *Songs for Her* and the more formal verse forms – the sizains and quatrains, with their hexasyllabic, octosyllabic, decasyllabic, and alexandrine lines, for instance – and its diction, as discovered in *Odes in Her Honor*, – the happy reader may find, as I have found and continue to find, that the poetry stands up solidly on its own, like a mushroom after a spring rain, or a British milestone. For example, here's something from *Songs for Her*:

> *I love you like you think*
> *And my crazy desire that grows,*
> *Like a mushroom in a field,*
> *Erects itself expressly like*
> *The Finger of a Term.*

Here's another example of pure Verlaine, without the nuance, Verlaine the poet we all musically know and love, from *Songs for Her* again:

> *After our nights of robust love*
> *I leave your arms strengthened,*
> *Your rich caress is the just caress*
> *With none of my flesh disappointed,*
> *Your love decants valiance*
> *Into all my being, like wine,*
> *And, alone, you know the science*
> *Of making my heart feel divine.*
>   *Love me,*
>   *For without you*
>   *I can do nothing,*
>   *I am nothing.*

Here is an example of more formal verse, with ever the ubiquitous Verlainian music, but little nuance, this time from *Odes in Her Honor*:

> *You were a great paramour*
> *In your manner, the only good one*
> *For it is your way, and nobody*
> *Was more miserable than you,*
> *After a crisis of good fortune*
> *That you carried honorably.*
>
> *Yes, you were like a heroine,*
> *And now you persist, a statue,*
> *Evermore beautiful on the ruins*
> *Of a hope that perpetuates*
> *In spite of evident Fortune,*

But you persist nonetheless!
....

Cast a glance of complaisance,
O strong woman, O saint, O queen,
On my fatal insufficiency,
Doubtless, of making you serene:
Ever saddened by withered time,
At least, smile on this old damned man.

In short summary, the poetry found in *Songs for Her* (published in 1891) and *Odes in Her Honor* (published in 1893) is somewhat contrary to the commonly held ideas of what Paul Verlaine's poetry is or "should be," in terms of nuance, but just as musically virtuosic or experimental as his earlier poetry was, which we all know and love. Because these are poems of mostly physical love, but also emotional love, between a middle-aged man and a woman (two women actually, just not *à trois*) – there is arguably little need for, and little use of, nuance. They are paeans to physical love.

As a sort of prosaic *envoi*, readers might be surprised, or intrigued, or impressed, to learn that in the same year that Verlaine published *Songs for Her,* he also finished and published *Bonheur,* the third book of his Catholic trilogy (the other two books being *Sagesse* and *Amour*). Also, in that same year, he published *My Hospitals,* an autobiographical prose work. One year later, in 1892, he published *Liturgies intimes*, another book of Catholic poetry. And, finally, in 1893, he published, *My Prisons,*[5] also an autobiographical prose work, as well as *Odes in Her Honor.* Sandwiching Catholic books with bawdy books. His writing didn't stop there, but we do (for now). Cheerio!

– Richard Robinson, February 2021

---

[5]*My Hospitals* and *My Prisons,* available in English translation by Sunny Lou Publishing, 2020.

Songs for Her

I

You're not at all virtuous,
I'm not at all jealous:
Taking life in stride, joyously,
That's still the sweetest way.

Long live love and long live us!

You practice and you possess
The most intelligent feats
And the most authentic tricks
Performed by honest peeps

And what indulgent cares you lavish on me!

Some yap about your age, –
You're not sixteen or twenty, –
But O your opulent corsage,
Your smiling eyes, as if singing,

And your kisses: O, they're stunning!

Be faithful to me if possible
And mostly if you want to be,
But stay often accessible
To my desire, your humble valet,

Content with a "come!" or a slap in the face.

"Huh? The time of prowess is passed!"
Say sots all about me.
They're wrong, for thanks to your caresses
It's still, it's always, my feat.
Long live us and long live love!

II

Good and savorous companion,
I've confided the care in you,
Definitively, of my person,
My last witness you are, *pardieu*!
Come here, that I might kiss you,
That I might hold you, long and hard;
Next to yours, my heart beats easily,
With love, 'til death do us part:
    Love me,
    For without you
    I can do nothing,
    I am nothing.

I go begging like a church rat,
And you have only your ten fingers;
The table often is not set
In our basements, beneath our rooves;
But our bed is never idle,
Always joyous, always fêted,
And I'm king of the *reich*
Of your gaiety, of your sanity!
    Love me,
    For without you
    I can do nothing,
    I am nothing.

After our nights of robust love
I leave your arms strengthened,
Your rich caress is the just caress
With none of my flesh disappointed,
Your love decants valiance
Into all my being, like wine,
And, alone, you know the science
Of making my heart feel divine.
    Love me,
    For without you

>   I can do nothing,
>   I am nothing.

Never mind your past, my belle,
And never mind mine, by golly!
I love you, with a faithful heart,
You've done nothing but good for me.
Let's combine, in our two poverties,
The pardon denied us;
I hold you, you embrace me –
To hell with those who gossip!
>   Love me,
>   For without you
>   I can do nothing,
>   I am nothing.

III

Wanting to escape you (to escape your love!
        But a poet is stupid.)
I scrammed one day, recently,
        I vanished;
Who was sheepish, and who was a fool,
        After a quarter of an hour?
And I came back, like a beggar
        That supplicates and weeps.

You pardoned me: but not long
        After the first time,
I made off like the South Wind,
        Just like the last time.
You looked for me, and dislodged me:
        Short and sweet was the inquest!
Who was content with this sweet stalking?
        Me then, your big idiot!

As here we are together again,
        What do say you, without feint, –
Let's not seek other nests anymore
        Than my, than your, embrace.
Despite my dreadful character,
        Despite your dreadful character,
Let's be happy forever:
        For the first, for the last time.

IV

Now, despite your feigned cruelty,
And the very false attitude
Of a filthy viciousness
That you, beast, are so proud of, –

I love your lasciviousness!

And although in spite of everything,
The too artificial disgust
Suggested to me by your smile
Which is, to my detriment and cost, –

Rouge on a mouse's white teeth!

I love you like you think,
And my crazy desire that grows,
Like a mushroom in a field,
Erects itself expressly like

The Finger of a Term.[6]

So, despite my feigned cruelty,
And the very false attitude
Of a worse viciousness
That I, beast, am so proud of, –

Love my simplicity.

---

[6]Term: a milestone.

V

Zon, flûte et basse
Zon, violin
       – Béranger

    Even the perverse nonchalances
        Of your dark eyes,
    Even, from the white listlessness
        Of those large haunches
    And a paunch, and two beautiful breasts
        With their proud outlines,

Everything perverts, everything converts all my designs,

    Even your dissembling,
        Bitten lips,
    Even the closely watched
        But poorly laid traps
    With so much delight, so many charms,
        So many alarms,

Everything perverts, everything converts my sad tears,

    And, Dear, ah! say it: Flutes and *zons*
        With my *chansons*
    That come a-troating, like nimble stags
        With agile gestes,
    Ah! say it then, Dear: Flute and *zon*!
        To my *chanson*,

And if I act the ass, eh well, throw me some hay!

VI

The season that advances
Forbids us the usage
Of summer customs,
The shiver of autumn
Already has us curling up
In bed, better fêted.

Fie on a morose summer,
Always the same stuff:
"I'm hot, you're hot, let's sleep!"
To sleep instead of live,
To grow bored like a book...
Here comes autumn, let's make nooky!

One inside the other, as we please,
Let's be hotter than embers
For winter's a-comin',
The two of us, body and soul, –
Let's be hotter than flames,
Let's be thicker than skin!

VII

I am poorer than ever
    And than anyone;
But I have your thick neck, your fresh arms,
    Your good fashion
Of making love, and the nimble
    And frivolous turn
And caress, day and night,
    Of your words.

I am rich in your eyes,
    And in your breasts,
Madly voluptuous nest,
    Ivory bed
Where my desire, weary on the one hand,
    Is reinvigorated
And for other gambols sets off again
    Braver yet...

Clearly you don't love me
    Like I love you,
I know how much you cheat on me
    In the extreme.
What does it matter given I live
    Only in your essence,
And that you hold my ravished senses
    Under your spell?

VIII

That your soul be black or white,
What matter? Your young and ivory skin
Is pink and white and yellow a bit.
That your perverse flesh smell good
Or not, what matter? So long as it rocks
That flesh of mine, name of God!

It rocks my crazy flesh,
Your crazy flesh does, my most
Sacred word! – and what about it?
And mine, thanks to yours,
Whatever reserve it have,
It profits from it, son of a whore!

As for our souls, say it, Madam,
You know, my soul and then your soul...
Do we give a damn? Not at all!
Only, we are on earth now,
Here below, on *terra firma,*
And not in heaven, but here below.

Now, being here below, we must profit
By the pleasure that passes so quickly
And the rapturous joy.
Let's make love again, my saucy slut,
Like the water flows, like the bird sings,
And so on, – love, nothing but.

IX

You struck me, it's ridiculous,
I beat you and it's awful:
I repent and you resent me for it.
That's fine, it's according to formula.

I needed only to remain calm
Under your friendly shower of slaps
By your hand expert in smacks,
Without asking why even.

And you, your right, your duty even,
At the risk of exhausting yourself,
Would be to continue
In extreme and supreme fashion...

But don't hold it against me
Even if it were a crime
To have made you my victim...
Say, – no more absolute refusals:

Beat the bejeebers out of me,
Little one, but then come kiss me,
No? Why the need to eternalize
So frivolous a quarrel.

To fall out longer than one instant,
The time it takes to pull a face,
What a peck on the cheek effaces,
Or on the mouth, while waiting

For better, – isn't that right, girl?
Promise me without kissing.
Is it agreed? Yes! Might I dare?
Let's go, – no more sour pusses!

X

Horrible night of insomnia!
– Without the blessed presence
Of your precious body next to me,
Without your mouth, so often kissed,
Although too cunning and
In entirely bad faith,

Without your mouth full of lies,
But so fresh when I think about it,
Which knows how to console me
Under the aspect and species
Of a strawberry – and, clever woman! –
With a very plausible conversation,

Above all without the pentacle
Of your senses and the miracle,
Multiple and one, flower and fruit,
Of your sorceress' hard eyes,
Hard and soft in your manner...
Good God! What a terrible night!

XI[7]

It is true, we are much too witty,
    Dear!
I think some evil has seized us,
    Dear,
To wage battle thus, body to body[8]
    Still,
Without repose and remorselessly
    Still!

No more, okay? of these purposeless
    Battles.
No more of these bad flutes,[9]
    That lute,
O that lute that assumes
    Such an air,
Always vibrant, dear tune
    In the air!

And we'll have no more wit then,
    Please!
You see what evil has seized us...
    Please.
Let's be good, quite simply
    You charmer,
Let's love each other amiably,
    My lover!

---

[7] The poem hinges on the extended metaphor of waging battle and making love.

[8] body to body: arm to arm combat, and making love.

[9] flutes: from French *flûte*, which has multiple meanings, of which the musical instrument, and a munitions cache. The pun is lost in translation.

XII

You drink, it's hideous! almost as much as I do.
I drink, it's shameless, almost more than you,
It is no longer what one could call a life...
Ah! woman, fool, a fool is he who trusts in her!

Men, bravo! they're proud and submissive,
One can trust them, behold they are friends!
We drink, but you, my ladies, drunkenness
Suits you less, – it transforms you into a tiger,

    Me all the more into a simple pig,
    Some ideal sot in my cups,
    Some idiocy to boot, some stupidity
    What's more, – but you, the laziness,

    The viciousness, the obstinacy,
    A little vice and a lot of choice,
    To be crazier, on my word!
    Than my madness so mad already.

    These reflections cost me a lot,
    But this evening I'm in a ravenous mood.
    Excuse me if my discourse is roguish,
    But this evening I've got a nasty humor.

    * * *

Bah, let's drink, not too much (if possible),
My mouth's a hole, yours is a riddle,
God knows how to recognize his own.
Courage! but above all else let's kiss, – come on!

XIII

    Are you blonde or brunette?
    Are they black or blue,
        Your eyes?
I know nothing about them, but I love their intense brightness,
And I adore the disorder in your hair.

    Are you soft or hard?
    Is it sensitive or mocking,
        Your heart?
I know nothing about it, but I thank nature
For having made your heart my master and conqueror.

    Faithful, or unfaithful?
    What does that matter,
        In fact
Given your beauty is disposed to crown my zeal
It always acts as a pledge for my dearest desire.

XIV

I don't love you all dressed up
And I detest the veil,
That obscures your eyes, my skies,
And I loathe the *"tournure"*[10]
Parody and caricature,
Of such sumptuous attractions as yours.

I'm hostile to your dress
Which hides and robs more or less
Your charms, fundamentally the best:
Your breasts, my dearest delights,
Your shoulders and the mischievousness
Of your enchanting calves.

Fie on a woman too well dressed!
I want you, my belle, in a nightshirt,
– Amiable veil, playful obstacle,
Altar cloth for a nourishing mass,
A cute flag, captured ceaselessly
Morning and night, night and morning.

---

[10]*tournure*: a play on words; it is both her physical aspect, height, etc. as well as an appurtenance of her dress.

XV

A woman's nightshirt is *ad hoc* armor
For dear combats and gay clashes,
With, so fresh, so white and armed,
Her two arms, all bare and joyous.

    Supreme attire,
    Always in style,
    It is you alone I love
    In all your finery.

When She draws near the bed,
The pride of two cambered breasts extends
And fills her linen, scented
By the only true perfume, her rapturous body.

    Supreme attire,
    Always in style,
    It is you alone I love
    In all your finery.

When she climbs into bed it is even
Better: under my hand the precious
Treasure of her croup shivers in
The redundant folds of the *batiste*.

    Supreme attire,
    Always in style,
    It is you alone I love
    In all your finery.

But when she has taken her place
Beside me, the humble serf of her beauty,
My joy is divine and diviner
To jostle her linen and honor!

    Supreme attire,

Always in style,
It is you alone I love
In all your finery.

XVI

Summer was not adorable
After that infernal winter
And what an unfavorable spring!
And autumn begins badly.
      Bah! we warmed ourselves
      By blending our souls together.

Poverty, our companion,
– We really could do without it, –
Vainly leads the campaign
During these long frozen months...
      We defy the intruder,
      His astuteness and his ruses.

And, rich in countless kisses,
– Our only opulence, trust me, –
What do we care if the weather be somber?
As long as it is sunny in me, in you,
      And that pleasure laughs
      At our indigence.

XVII

I'm no longer one of those philosophical souls,
And it's not morality you pride yourself on,
Two admirable conditions for love
As we understand it, which is without tower[11]
And no stupid convenances or boundaries,
Just hot, laughing – and damn all hypocritical usages!

>   Let's love gaily
>   And frankly

I recognized that virtue, as far as Woman is concerned,
Is dupery and the better part of them have
Reason to forgo it, taking us for examples:
So that it is very fine to do as do
The good beasts of the earth and the celestials,
Isn't that right? prompt sparrows, isn't that right, agile stags?

>   Let's love strongly
>   Until death.

Follow my good advice and be amusing.
If possible, be even more so, and represent
To yourself that it is your "essential law" to charm us.
And that the flower is not made to be closed
Any more than our hearts and senses, O our beautiful friends...
Head held high, clear senses, your "pudors" asleep.

>   Let's love duly
>   And vigorously!

---

[11]tower: in the courtly romance sense.

XVIII

If you really want me to, divine Ignoramus,
I will act like a man who knows nothing else
Than to caress you with an errant hand,
With the expert *geste* of the worst good-for-nothing,

If you really want me to, divine Ignoramus.

Let's be scandalous without annoying each other
Any more than the stag and his bitch in authentic woods.
Shame, let's send it packing.
Let's exaggerate even and, if not cynical,

Let's be scandalous without annoying each other.

Above all, let's not talk about literature.
To hell with readers, authors, publishers
Above all! Let's leave ourselves to our nature
In the charming oblivion of all pudor,

And, O! let's not talk about literature.

Enjoy then and sleep, do you want to? This will be
Our first and last function,
Our only and our double virtue,
Unique conscience, unique light,

Enjoy then and sleep, my love, do you want to?

XIX

Your laughter lights up my old heart
Like a lantern in a cave
Where such vanquishing vintages age:
Aï, Beaune, Sauternes, Graves.

Your laughter lights up my old heart.

Your voice clarions in my soul:
Like a signal to run to the fire...
... Of your eyes, effectually all flame, –
I'll go there, blessed name of Names!

Your voice clarions in my soul.

Your manner, your *meneo*[12],
Your chic, your shape, your... what do I know,
All tell me: "Come here." – *Prodeo*[13]
(O these memories from grade school!)

Your manner! your *meneo!*

Your bosom, your haunches, your gesture,
And all the rest, odor and freshness
And warmth insinuate in me: rest!
As if I could rest in your ravenous bed!

Your bosom! your haunches! your gesture!

---

[12]*meneo*: potentially from Portuguese or Spanish, possibly from Latin, first person singular indicative: I wiggle, I wag.

[13]*Prodeo*: Latin for I advance, I move forward.

XX

You believe in reading coffee grounds,
In presages, in a roll of the dice:
Me, I believe only in your big eyes.

You believe in fairy tales,
In nefarious days, in dreams,
Me, I believe only in your lies.

You believe in a vague God,
In some special saint,
In such *Ave* to ward off such evil.

I believe only in the blue and pink
Hours you deal out to me
In the voluptuousness of our white nights!

And so deep is my faith
In all I believe in
That I live only for you now!

XXI

When you ferret your fleas
    It's very funny.
What ruses, what schemes!
    I love this scene.
It's devilishly attractive
    And my heart throbs
With a throbbing in anticipation
    Of some other frolic.

Under a taut shirt
    Held out, with both hands,
Your eyes scan the expanse
    Between two firm breasts.
You always return empty handed,
    Moreover, from this game.
No matter, it troubles and confuses me
    Your sport, and not a little!

Stop looking so foolishly
    defeated.
Come reward your charming body
    With other entertainment
Than an unprofitable chase
    Oe'r the hills, and across the vales.
You'll be victorious, I promise...
    Unless I prevail!

XXII

I dreamt of you last night:
You were ecstatic in a thousand poses
And billed and cooed a ton of things...

And me, as one savors a fruit,
I was kissing you on the mouth
And a little all over, mountain, valley, and plain.

I had a young man's elasticity,
A truly admirable spring in my step:
Great god, what breath and loins!

And you, dear, for your part
What loins, what breath, what
Elasticity of a gazelle...

On waking, my dream was more poignant
And more perfect in your arms, –
Exactly the same banquet!

XXIII

I have no luck with women,
And, given my age as a man,
I have not run into, in short,
But loathsome shrews recently.

It is true that I'm strident
Myself and have a completely
Revolting character as well,
Maybe worse, perchance.

My women friends were frivolous,
You are yourself a bit,
This dreadful confession
Let's keep it between us, dear.

It's true I was a womanizer,
I am still, maybe:
This confession dishonors me.
Sometimes I'm horrified at myself.

Enough! for all that let's
Stay lovers, given, in short,
You, a good girl, and me, a fine fellow,
We love each other, admit it.

XXIV

Even though she's your best friend,
It's a farce to deceive her
Excessively, without considering her feelings
A bit, though our moments are good,

    Our moments are good!

I make comparisons, just like you
Cuckolding your other lover,
And I must say that your system
Of cuckolding him is charming.

    Your system is charming!

My pleasure is all the more culpable
(But more exquisite, thanks to your competition)
While she proves herself quite capable
And extremely skilled in things of love,

    But, without your competition?

Let's fool her good then, for she fools us
Also perhaps, everyone's so mischievous
And it's not like we're breaking a pact.
Let's deceive them *both*. No petty remorse!

    Let's be really mischievous!

XXV

I was a mystic and now I am not anymore
(Women have taken everything away from me),
Not without holding an absolute respect
For the ideal I had to betray.

But women have taken everything away from me!

I went praying to God in my childhood
(Today it is you who have me on my knees).
I was full of faith, candid hope,
Saintly charity, with such pure sweet zeal.

But today you have me at your knees!

With you, the woman becomes THE master again,
An all-powerful and tyrannical master,
But how insidious! feigning to allow anything
To arrive at such a satanic end...

O blessed days – when I was that mystic!

Odes in Her Honor

I[14]

You were a great paramour
In your fashion, the only good one
For it is your way, and nobody
Was more miserable than you,
After a crisis of good fortune
That you carried honorably.

Yes, you were like a heroine,
And now you persist, a statue,
Evermore beautiful on the ruins
Of a hope that perpetuates
In spite of your evident Fortune,
But you persist nonetheless!

For that, I love you and admire
You even more than I love you
Perhaps, and it is a supreme
Pride for me to be better or worse
Than he who does every evil,
To be at your feet trembling, feal![15]

Use me, for I am your thing;
My love goes, your humble slave,
Ready for anything that your
Hard, suave will might propose,
Prompt to enjoy, prompt to endure,
Prompt for anything, save dying!

To die in my body and soul,
I'll accept that if it's your whim.

---

[14]This poem appeared in the *Chat Noir* journal, April 9, 1892. (As did several others in this book of poetry.)

[15]Feal: as in fealty.

When I must cease to exist
Entirely, make a sign, woman,
But how might my love cease to exist?
It can only last forever.

Cast a glance of complaisance,
O strong woman, O saint, O queen,
On my fatal insufficience,
Doubtless, of making you serene:
Ever saddened by withered time,
At least, smile on this old damned man.

II

Let calumny say what it will,
Lie, contradict, deny, renege,
And even worse let gossip,
Which gives only to take back again,
And which borrows only to resell...
Ah! Let it do, say, what it will!

Do and say, cowards and sots,
False fine folk, fake mascots,
Aspic, viperous tongues;
They do hypocritical acts,
They speak, full of their merits,
Ill of you, which exasperates me.

Me who esteems you and venerates you
Above all else on this earth,
Esteems you and venerates you, my belle,
With the mad love that I devote,
To you, good and not too pouty,
Admitting me to your bed, my devotee!

But you, you disdain these intrigues
More than your destinies,
Great heart, glorious martyr,
Hover above your rancors
Against these men or those women.
Bah! Let them do, say, what they will!

Bah! Do as you want to, my belle,
Good woman, – faithful, unfaithful, –
As all your life you have done, but
Always, everywhere, be good,
And fear nothing from anyone,
Although they have envy and hatred.

And then you have me, if you grant me

A bit of those mercies fitting for
An honest old fuddy-duddy.
You have me, dear, to defend you,
To please you, if you want to see
And hear me, though ugly and dumb.

III

The spreading of your arms is dear to me, almost dearer
            Than some other spreading:
Strong sea and how beautiful and how fine in the flesh,
            What an allure is yours!

O breasts, my great pride, my immense happiness,
            Pure, white, joy and caress,
Voluptuousness for my eyes and hands and heart
            That beats, drunk on you.

Armpits, with fine short hair, that waft a heady perfume
            That I plunge into,
Neck thick like honey, scented with ambergris, that a
            God makes much better than in a dream,

Freshness of arms finally, fallen asleep and dreamy
            Around my shoulders,
Palpitant and so sweet in the embrace of my fervors
            With all their great roles to play,

That I don't know what cries in me, full of pleasure,
            Mad pleasure, fully chaste,
That I cannot fully satisfy the desire
            That my soul is filled with.

That in more languorous and ardent kisses
            On your glorious bust,
Not without a feeling that is a little sad in
            An ecstasy so august!

And now towards the white shadow – and black a bit,
            Love, it can distend
Its proud game lower and more intimate
            Since then naïve and tender!

IV

The saint, the patron![16] is above all venerated
In our northern climes and all the land
I half come from, Lorraine and the Ardennes.
She was courageous, gentle, and died a virgin
And martyr. Now we must burn a pretty candle
On this day of your feast and play some prank
Also perhaps in her honor, O my pagan!

You're not a virgin, alas! But still a martyr
Not for God, but those you liked (what have they to laugh about?)
On account of your bleeding heart that stayed sublime.
Courageous you are, poor, dear, adored,
To endure such inordinate pain
With that self-esteem that decorates a victim,
With that joyous and magnanimous forgiveness.

And sweet? Ah yes! Despite so vivid an allure,
So strong and so rude sometimes. Sweet and naïve
Like your childish voice with the strains of a peasant.
Sweet to the poor, and naïve towards all, and how good
Beneath an often brutal exterior that surprises you,
You, the people, but that I quickly learned the arcana of!

Sweet and naïve and good, exquisite soul that planes
Above all stupid, or ferocious, prejudice,
Above the hypocrisy and the vicious *cant*
And the deceiving jargon and the fetid slang,
In the pure region where hatred is ignored, and
Where rancor expires, there where pure love displays
Its candid[17] banner in the whiteness of the sky.
O infinitely splendid resignation!

On this day of your feast, and despite our frivolous

---

[16]saint... patron: Saint Philomena; her feast day is August 11.

[17]candid: in the sense white.

Preoccupations, less culpable than foolish,
With kisses expressly redoubled, and the refrain,
More gentle still than excessive in nimble words,
But let's reflect, let's think on the fine celestial
Beings, so that after death or, alas, after yours,
The survivor prays for the decedent, O my Christian!

V

"When I chat with you peacefully
It's really charming, you chat with me so peacefully!

When I dispute with you and make reproaches,
You dispute with me, it's amusing, and you make reproaches.

If I happened, alas, to cause you some infidelity,
O misery! You run about town to cause me some infidelity.

And if I was, for a length of time, faithful,
You remain, for that same length of time, faithful.

When I'm happy, you show yourself more happy
Still, and I'm more happy again! to see you so happy.

When I cry, you cry by my side.
When I'm insistent, you come very kindly to my side.

When I swoon, then you swoon,
And I swoon even more to see you also swoon.

Ah! Tell me, when I die, will you die too, will you?"
She: "Because I loved you more, I will die more than you."

And I woke up from this colloquy.
Alas! It was a dream (if not a dream, then what?) this colloquy.

VI

But after the marvels
That have no parallel
In shoulder and breast,
We need another mode
To raise a pretty ode
To the glorious pelvis.

We must celebrate the white
Suppleness of the haunch
And its mat breadth,
We must sing the opulent belly
And its sublime curve
Toward the sex eater.

How chastely, how prettily
Even, it decorates
And protects sufficiently,
The shadow that rests on
Divine things, slightly morose,
Thickly pleated, curtains,

Adorable Teutates,[18]
More amiable Saturn,
The dear anthropophagus
That wants, at sacrifices,
Not the blood of heifers
But the milk of my flesh.

We will chant then
The blonde groin and its ambergris
Escape at the heart of the Saint...
But let's set down the lyre now
And adhere to a reasonable
And succinct delirium, okay?

---

[18]Teutates: a Celtic god worshipped in ancient Britain and Gaul.

No! Mad, barmy, orgiastic,
Like Apaches in kayaks,
Drunk on rum:
We are not the man
For erudite Sodom when
There is a Woman.

VII

Fifi woke up. At around daybreak you wished me
Bonjour with two kisses, and Pépia, poor little thing,
Hid his head under his wing again and
Silenced for a moment his soft ritornello.
Whereupon I gave you, in exchange, a kiss,
Multiform, ubiquitous, and which was planted
From the soles of your feet to the tips of your dark hair
With stations[19] in between of lightning and dark clouds,
A game (for you laughed) ridiculously sweet;
And, brusquely, I pushed my knees between yours,
Immediately resting on them and, leaning in towards your mouth,
I was brutal without you seeming too timid,
For you were thanking me with a wet look.
It was then that Fifi woke up suddenly.

The darling companion! Like fine fellows
Who are not made envious by another's happiness,
He saluted my triumph with two trilled salvoes
That with all his heart he launched heavensward.

He hopped, cocky, like a guy throwing out his chest,
Acclaiming a justly honored victor,
And the dawn, showing through the windowpanes,
Honestly attested that we had just made love.

---

[19]stations: places of rest.

VIII

Thighs thick but tapering,
Tender but firm below;
Above, hard but soft,
Muscular and chubby;

Thighs so fine, so kissed
From birth and since,
Whiter than the tea rose,[20]
Occupying my thoughts.

Knees, little angel caps
Swelling with due leanness;
Bounding, fussing calves
In white socks, shy of filth;

Your feet tippy-toed in order
To lift you, so I could kiss you,
Me, to lift you and carry you
To bed, your pretty feet

Buskined by soft ivory
Ankles that their freshness scents;
Delicate toes, frail pink
Slightly tawny at the heel,

With thick skin for walking,
But what! A dear body needs not
A firm base and strong supports
To protect my Ark?

Ark of fear and caresses
Where I enter, my wrongs atoned,
As one enters heaven. Divine
Feet, fine knees, good thighs!

---

[20]tea rose: a hybrid rose that smells like Chinese black tea. Color ranges from pastel white, pink, yellow...

IX

You were often cruel,
Even unjust sometimes,
But what about it, O my belle,
Given in you alone I trust,

And because I'm your thing.

You cheat on me with Pierre,
Louis, *et cætera punctum,*
I know, but, hey! s'none of my business,
I'm merely the humble factotum

Of your gay or morose humor.

If you should beat me,
Slap me, scratch me, you're
The master of our Penates,
And me, the cuckold, the trodden,

I'm content, and all is rosy.

   And then, damn! I opine
   That to see me thus, under
   Your thumb, you'll end up divine,
   By lovin' me thus, for

One grows attached to one's thing.

X

And now, for the Buttocks!
I want you to confess,
Muse, these mine treasures
For which, – trust me on this –
I would give one hundred lives
And, if rich, all my gold
And so much more besides.

But before the *cantate* –
That my soul and prostate
And my blood in arrest –
Are going to sing in praise
Of her dear Ass, which the angel...
O fallen! would first salute,
And then he would adore,

Let's plant slow kisses
On the pretty delights of
What's beneath your knees,
Supple Chinese paper,
Fine tendons, fine traces
Of vein with no noticeable
Pulse, it is so smooth!

And now, for the Buttocks!
Goddesses' goddesses,
Flesh's flesh, beauty's beauty,
The only beauty that touches us
Outside your breasts maybe,
Excitedly, always new
Divine pulp, nourishing skin!

They are nearly oval,
Nearly round. Opal,
Amber, pink (very little)
They blend, fuse together

In a white mat that responds
To the black, rose color
Of a line down the middle.

Goddesses' goddesses!
Of reposes in jubilation,
Of calm gaieties,
Artful dimples
As well as nice smiles,
Some perversity
With what majesty!...

And when the time comed
To join my fate
To your feted destiny,
I can go fearlessly
And attempt an embrace
On the flip side:
The competition is on!

I stand up, and I press one
One bun after the other
In my happy hands.
All their ardor gives,
Their vigor is the aide,
To help with the hymens
From morning to midnight...

And then there are her loins,
Ample, on edge, that love
Invites to the only
Transports this world needs,
It is her pudgy back and a world,
Warm satin, white lightning,
Troubling undulations.

And then the nape finally,
Which, to avoid shivering,

One needs be a eunuch,
The nape of a damnatrix,
The crazy dominatrix,
With its naughty shivers
Which we recognize.

O nape of a proxenete,
Vaguely dishonest,
And vaguely chaste.
Shivers, – a pretty symbol
Of the veils of the Idol
Of this charming temple,
Doubly precious shivers!

XI

Rich belly that never has carried,
Opulent breasts that never have fed,
Arms fresh and plump, pure with servile care,

Beautiful neck that never bent but for the weight
Of slow kisses on every cherished place,
Chin where idleness stands out,

Mouth, bright red, whence words
Never escaped that I didn't love, like birds
Idle and gay – what a nest of delights!

A turned-up nose smelling only the scents
Of her robust health, eyes lighter than black,
Darker than brown, indulgently complicit,

Forehead not too thoughtful – so much the better,
Long black hair whose great silky wave
Ventures heavily down to the small of her back,

Superb croup smitten with leisure,
Except for works of paramount pleasure,
Except for gay battles where it brings up the rear,

Legs finally, valiant only
In the pleasant act, at the right moment,
Squeezing my chest or kicking in the air,

Then, at rest – thighs, knees, calves –
Smelling like ambergris, and white as milk:
– Such is the portrait of my naked woman.

XII

But Her head, Her head!
Mad, unique tempest
Of indignant injustice,
Of furious falsehood,
Visions of butchery
And igneous vengeance.

Then the exquisite calm,
Of a sun-filled space,
A dove above the abyss,
All good thoughts,
Caressed and cradled
For a sublime awakening.

A force of nature
Magnificently hard
And so soft, Her head,
Adored phenomenon
O of my Philomène[21]
The head, the one celebration!

And look just how beautiful it is
That head, rebellious
Against literature as well as
To the art of the brush
And ferocious chisel, –
Look, future races!

For I want to tell the Angels
About this dearest of visages,
The hair black as shade
Where the waves might pass,
Pure, cold, deep,
Under a lowering somber sky.

---

[21]Philomène Boudin, for whom these odes are written.

The Divine small forehead
Knitted into a quarrel,
The cute turned-up nose
That takes flight and ironizes,
The mouth whence Her word
Departs, precise, concise.

But unfailingly bewitching,
Which wounds and caresses
My obedient soul,
Submissive, adulterous,
O voice of a dominatrix,
O almighty voice!...

And O on that mouth
More bitter than wild,
More wild than tender,
More tender than ordinary,
A Kiss seems to attend
The fundamentally debonaire prince,

And all that is lit up by
The encompassing regard
Of two beautiful eyes, like embers,
Brown with some flame,
Deceitful with some soul
And some heart, not displeasing

To us jealous, my queen,
My noble sovereign,
Who holds me enthralled,
That beautiful and good
And bad head, – and the crown
Of the throne, your Shoulders.

XIII

Our meals are charming although humble,
Thanks to the profound art of yours of accommodating leftovers
From yesterday's roast or some recent stew
Of mincemeat and ragout, as not found on God's table.

The wine bottle is label-less, – for what good is glory?
And given it's been uncorked, shouldn't we drink it?
As for bread, as if we haven't eaten our fill already,
That it seems excellent to us – seems to tell me a story.

The legumes are nearly next to nothing, and the cheese:
We eat it like royalty, as would seem to be our habit.
As for the fruit, what do we care for the season's first,
Provided we have something at this truly frugal feast.

But the triumph, at least for me, is the salad:
How she digs into it! without ever feeling ill,
More ravenously than a dead Tragaldabas[22],
And I can't get over how pretty she looks at those frolics.

And the coffee, which I don't much care for personally,
How she loves it, my good friends, what an affair!
I'm amused and I'm happy for her, really!
Besides, I know that at night I'll profit thereby.

I know quite well that sleep will evade her lips
And her eyes will still be lit by a bit of excitement
From the drop of rum imbibed while gaily clinking glasses
With me, gentle presage of a much more charming bump.

---

[22]Tragaldabas, presumably in reference to the main character of a comic opera by the same name, by Auguste Vacquerie, from around 1848.

XIV

We are well suited for each other;
However, when you met me,
Dragging around my last difficulties
Of a serious man and good apostle,
The ruin of a Christian still,
A pagan philosopher already,

Weighed down by doctrine and scruple,
(All a bit decomposed),
But fundamentally very well disposed
For the tavern and debauchery,
In a word, a sot among sots
Of that sort of virgin,

You had some trouble in the conquest,
– And what I mean by this word
Is your absolute triumph, –
If not of my heart, of my head;
I don't say of my body,
Which you had at "*Salut!*"

But since we sympathized,
Since our spirits were kindred,
And from then on what a perfect accord
Between those gals, our two souls,
Those gals and our guys
Of wit, all square and all round!

You're still simple, but complicated,
And me, I'm naïve a hundred fold,
Our experiences in bed
And our marked ignorance
By way of subtle feelings,
All this makes us agreeable

To each other! despite, in crises,

Angers set afoot quite quickly,
Dark humors, soon rose-colored,
And, my God, what a pile of stupidities
That one atoned for, in order to satisfy
Madame and Monsieur, with a kiss!

We must persevere, my petite!
We must, my dear, continue,
Even if it means killing ourselves
Sometimes, to be resuscitated finally,
We must remain a couple, really,
Good heart and bad rascal.

XV

When you tell me the stories
Of your bitch of a life too,
My tears fall thick, heavy, as from
Fountains into basins,
And my long condolent sighs
Combine with your slow recitations.

You told me your first loves:
A country girl with the guys
Then a city girl with her misdemeanors
And the usual and mutual
Remorseless betrayals
On both sides, as if by mutual agreement.

Suddenly a quick caprice,
Ripening by habit into a wild
Passion, like the humble scion
Growing quickly into a palm tree
That a desert wind would shake
In some green landscape.

Faithful you, unfaithful the other,
You grievous, lax, furious
Finally, drunk on the wine
Of vice, soaring on a wing
Your heart like a wounded eagle,
But unable to escape your past...

I hear you, and all my pity,
All my admiration,
An ineffable feeling,
Goes out to you, by some route,
If not that of a pure love
Which would suffer, dear, in its turn,

Which will suffer, I'm afraid,

Which already suffers, as you know,
You, sometimes bad to excess,
But charming too, like a saint,
Towards this one, me, your good ole lover,
The last one, huh, probably?

XVI

I'm not jealous of your past, dear,
And I even love you more and admire you for it.
It shows your big heart and the unfaded glory
Of a tender but strong, but also impetuous love.

Because you had fear of neither death nor life,
And, until that proud autumn reflected
In the tumultuous days of your prime beauty,
Your touching sob, a sublime honor, has stayed with you.

Your touching sob that your endearing laugh condoled
Like a more manly brother, and those two good geniuses
Have blessed you in my eyes with infinite virtues
Which my love, proud as a peacock, took advantage of

And preens itself on order to adore you in the mystical sense:
Consolations, vows, respect, at the same time as
Humble caresses and the *ex-voto* homages
From my flesh for that valiant body of yours, the heroic temple

Where so many passions as in a Pantheon,
Rancors, pardons, rages, and holy lust
Hold their cult, respecting the pure form
And powerful contour profaned by Phaon.

Think on Phaon in order to forget him in my gentler
And more faithful embrace, lover of an afternoon,
Of an extreme, but not lukewarm, afternoon, –
For look at me, all full of ecstasies and fear.

Go on, I love you.... more than the other: you must forget him.
You: smile at me at least between two confidences,
Wounded Amazon warrioress of stunning imprudences
Who awakens in the arms of a stout old equerry.

XVII

"You're stubborn!" – "And I'm taking you
To the country." Thus spoke
Two lovers of whose prattle
More than a follow-up word was heard.

I'm rather afraid that those lovers
Sounded a lot like us last week,
Like Tircis and Clymène,
Alas! in too savorous words.

But because there is still time,
Because there is time still,
Let's not be upset anymore then,
On the contrary, let's tone down

Our anger, all the while grumbling,
A little for form's sake, but
In an enormous, horrible outburst,
Exchanging big kisses.

O my tough and good companion,
Enough, say it, of misunderstandings,
If you don't mind me saying so, for I must –
Now, "I'm taking you to the country."

XVIII

O you triumphant over two "Rivals"
(To sound highfalutin' about it),
You were ironic, – they... late[23] –
And you employed no more subtle effort
Than was needed to ensure you were –
Their better, thanks to that habit

You have, without trying, to please
More than is needed, my caprices.
Now, I will play you a tune
All scented with iris and ambergris
Although holding in triple horror
All hostile or complicit perfume,

Save only your odor, yours,
Fresh and hot effluvium, sea breeze
And the breeze, under the sun, of prairies
Not without some bitter savor
To season it, salt and pepper it,
So urgent is it, my numb heart,

My heart, but not my bravura,
In matters of love! You would resuscit-
Ate a deadman, arousing him for
The diversion to which Venus says: *Sit!*
Yes, my heart still pitter-patters
In close combat, but with what fear!

Fear to lose you if the spell
Of arms had betrayed your clouts,
Fear of you even, fear even
Of so many sulks and pouts.
As for the other two, O la la! You
Need not think on it, you won!

---

[23]late: i.e., defunct.

Iris, ambergris, thus have I dedicated
– My memory is good – these verses
To your gay and proud conquest
Over somniferous rivals.
Not that they have the gift, so pure,
So dear: of smelling like your skin!

XIX

They tell me that you cheat on me.
For starters, what is it to them?
Dear frivolous one, that you break
An oath you did not make?

They tell me that you're vicious
Towards me, – me, who am so good!
You, vicious! Let some other sing
This refrain quite far from being good.

Vicious, you who always offer me
An ever-amusing smile,
You, my queen, who from your coffers
Ever expose your treasures.

They tell me and think they're right
In saying, O you, that you don't love me?
Who cares, I have your smile at night,
And then, – you would not love me?

You don't love me? And the grace
And strength of your beauty,
You give them to me, large and fat
And voluptuous beauty.

You don't love me? And even if
You didn't, what can I do?
"If you don't love me, I love you."
– But you love me, in the act.

Chansons pour Elle (French)

I

Tu n'es pas du tout vertueuse,
Je ne suis pas du tout jaloux!
C'est de se la couler heureuse
Encor le moyen le plus doux.

Vive l'amour et vivent nous!

Tu possèdes et tu pratiques
Les tours les plus intelligents
Et les trucs les plus authentiques
A l'usage des braves gens,

Et tu m'as quels soins indulgents!

D'aucuns clabaudent sur ton âge
Qui n'est plus seize ans ni vingt ans,
Mais ô ton opulent corsage,
Tes yeux riants, comme chantants,

Et ô tes baisers épatants!

Sois-moi fidèle si possible
Et surtout si cela te plaît,
Mais reste souvent accessible
À mon désir, humble valet

Content d'un «viens!» ou d'un soufflet.

«Hein? passé le temps des prouesses!»
Me disent les sots d'alentour.
Ça, non, car grâce à tes caresses
C'est encor, c'est toujours mon tour.

Vivent nous et vive l'amour!

II

Compagne savoureuse et bonne
À qui j'ai confié le soin
Définitif de ma personne,
Toi mon dernier, mon seul témoin,
Viens çà, chère, que je te baise,
Que je t'embrasse long et fort,
Mon coeur près de ton coeur bat d'aise
Et d'amour pour jusqu'à la mort:
    Aime-moi,
    Car, sans toi,
    Rien ne puis,
    Rien ne suis.

Je vais gueux comme un rat d'église
Et toi tu n'as que tes dix doigts;
La table n'est pas souvent mise
Dans nos sous-sols et sous nos toits;
Mais jamais notre lit ne chôme,
Toujours joyeux, toujours fêté
Et j'y suis le roi du royaume
De ta gaîté, de ta santé!
    Aime-moi,
    Car, sans toi,
    Rien ne puis,
    Rien ne suis.

Après nos nuits d'amour robuste
Je sors de tes bras mieux trempé,
Ta riche caresse est la juste,
Sans rien de ma chair de trompé,
Ton amour répand la vaillance
Dans tout mon être, comme un vin,
Et, seule, tu sais la science
De me gonfler un coeur divin.
    Aime-moi,
    Car, sans toi,

   Rien ne puis,
   Rien ne suis.

Qu'importe ton passé, ma belle,
Et qu'importe, parbleu! le mien:
Je t'aime d'un amour fidèle
Et tu ne m'as fait que du bien.
Unissons dans nos deux misères
Le pardon qu'on nous refusait
Et je t'étreins et tu me serres
Et zut au monde qui jasait!
   Aime-moi,
   Car, sans toi,
   Rien ne puis,
   Rien ne suis.

III

Voulant te fuir (fuir ses amours!
      Mais un poète est bête),
J'ai pris, l'un de ces derniers jours,
      La poudre d'escampette.
Qui fut penaud, qui fut nigaud
      Dès après un quart d'heure?
Et je revins en mendigot
      Qui supplie et qui pleure.

Tu pardonnas: mais pas longtemps
      Depuis la fois première
Je filais, pareil aux autans,
      Comme la fois dernière.
Tu me cherchas, me dénichas;
      Courte et bonne, l'enquête!
Qui fut content du doux pourchas?
      Moi donc, ta grosse bête!

Puisque nous voici réunis,
      Dis, sans ruse et sans feinte,
Ne nous cherchons plus d'autres nids
      Que ma, que ton étreinte.
Malgré mon caractère affreux,
      Malgré ton caractère
Affreux, restons toujours heureux:
      Fois première et dernière.

IV

    Or, malgré ta cruauté
    Affectée, et l'air très faux
    De sale méchanceté
    Dont, bête, tu te prévaux

    J'aime ta lasciveté !

    Et quoiqu'en dépit de tout
    Le trop factice dégoût
    Que me dicte ton souris
    Qui m'est, à mes dams et coût,

Rouge aux crocs blancs de souris ! —

    Je t'aime comme l'on croit,
    Et mon désir fou qui croît,
    Tel un champignon des prés,
    S'érige ainsi que le Doigt

    D'un Terme là tout exprès.

    Donc, malgré ma cruauté
    Affectée, et l'air très faux
    De pire méchanceté,
    Dont, bête, je me prévaux.

    Aime ma simplicité.

V

Zon, flûte et basse
Zon, violin
      – Béranger

   Jusques aux pervers nonchaloirs
      De ces yeux noirs,
   Jusques, depuis ces flemmes blanches
      De larges hanches
   Et d'un ventre et de beaux seins
      Aux fiers dessins,

Tout pervertit, tout convertit tous mes desseins

   Jusques à votre menterie,
      Bouche fleurie,
   Jusques aux pièges mal tendus
      Tant attendus,
   De tant d'appas, de tant de charmes.
      De tant d'alarmes,

Tout pervertit, tout avertit mes tristes larmes,

   Et, chère, ah! dis: Flûtes et zons
      À mes chansons
   Qui vont brâmant, tels des cerfs prestes
      Aux gestes lestes,
   Ah! dis donc, Chère: Flûte et zon!
      À ma chanson,

Et si je fais l'âne, eh bien, donne-moi du son!

VI

La saison qui s'avance
Nous baille la défense
D'user des us d'été,
Le frisson de l'automne
Déjà nous pelotonne
Dans le lit mieux fêté.

Fi de l'été morose,
Toujours la même chose:
«J'ai chaud, t'as chaud, dormons!»
Dormir au lieu de vivre
S'ennuyer comme un livre...
Voici l'automne, aimons!

L'un dans l'autre, à notre aise,
Soyons pires que braise
Puisque s'en vient l'hiver,
Tous les deux, corps et âme,
Soyons pires que flamme,
Soyons pires que chair!

VII

Je suis plus pauvre que jamais
      Et que personne;
Mais j'ai ton cou gras, tes bras frais.
      Ta façon bonne
De faire l'amour, et le tour
      Leste et frivole,
Et la caresse, nuit et jour,
      De ta parole.

Je suis riche de tes beaux yeux.
      De ta poitrine,
Nid follement voluptueux,
      Couche ivoirine
Où mon désir, las d'autre part.
      Se ravigore
Et pour d'autres ébats repart
      Plus brave encore...

Sans doute tu ne m'aimes pas
      Comme je t'aime,
Je sais combien tu me trompes
      Jusqu'à l'extrême.
Que me fait, puisque je ne vis
      Qu'en ton essence,
Et que tu tiens mes sens ravis
      Sous ta puissance?

VIII

Que ton âme soit blanche ou noire,
Que fait? Ta peau de jeune ivoire
Est rose et blanche et jaune un peu.
Elle sent bon, ta chair, perverse
Ou non, que fait? puisqu'elle berce
La mienne de chair, nom de Dieu!

Elle la berce, ma chair folle,
Ta folle de chair, ma parole
La plus sacrée! — et que donc bien!
Et la mienne, grâce à la tienne,
Quelque réserve qui la tienne,
Elle s'en donne, nom d'un chien!

Quant à nos âmes, dis, Madame,
Tu sais, mon âme et puis ton âme,
Nous en moquons-nous? Que non pas!
Seulement nous sommes au monde.
Ici-bas, sur la terre ronde,
Et non au ciel, mais ici-bas.

Or, ici-bas, faut qu'on profite
Du plaisir qui passe si vite
Et du bonheur de se pâmer,
Aimons, ma petite méchante,
Telle l'eau va, tel l'oiseau chante,
Et tels, nous ne devons qu'aimer.

IX

Tu m'as frappé, c'est ridicule,
Je l'ai battue et c'est affreux:
Je m'en repens et tu m'en veux.
C'est bien, c'est selon la formule.

Je n'avais qu'à me tenir coi
Sous l'aimable averse des gifles
De ta main experte en mornifles,
Sans même demander pourquoi.

Et toi, ton droit, ton devoir même,
Au risque de t'exténuer,
Il serait de continuer
De façon extrême et suprême...

Seulement, ô ne m'en veux plus,
Encore que ce fût un crime
De t'avoir faite ma victime...
Dis, plus de refus absolus,

Bats-moi, petite, comme plâtre,
Mais ensuite viens me baiser,
Pas? quel besoin d'éterniser
Une querelle trop folâtre.

Pour se brouiller plus d'un instant,
Le temps de nous faire une moue
Qu'éteint un bécot sur la joue,
Puis sur la bouche en attendant

Mieux encor, n'est-ce pas, gamine?
Promets-le-moi sans biaiser.
C'est convenu? Oui? Puis-je oser?
Allons, plus de ta grise mine!

X

L'horrible nuit d'insomnie!
— Sans la présence bénie
De ton cher corps près de moi,
Sans ta bouche tant baisée
Encore que trop rusée
En toute mauvaise foi,

Sans ta bouche tout mensonge,
Mais si franche quand j'y songe,
Et qui sait me consoler
Sous l'aspect et sous l'espèce
D'une fraise — et, bonne pièce! —
D'un très plausible parler,

Et surtout sans le pentacle
De tes sens et le miracle
Multiple est un, fleur et fruit,
De tes durs yeux de sorcière,
Durs et doux à ta manière...
Vrai Dieu! la terrible nuit!

XI

Vrai, nous avons trop d'esprit.
      Chérie!
Je crois que mal nous en prit,
      Chérie!
D'ainsi lutter corps à corps
      Encore!
Sans repos et sans remords
      Encore!

Plus, n'est-ce pas? de ces luttes
      Sans but,
Plus de ces mauvaises flûtes.
      Ce luth,
Ô ce luth de bien se faire
      Tel air,
Toujours vibrant, chanson hère
      Dans l'air!

Et n'ayons plus d'esprit,
      T'en prie!
Tu vois que mal nous en prit...
      T'en prie.
Soyons bons tout bêtement,
      Charmante,
Aimons-nous aimablement
      M'amante!

XII

Tu bois, c'est hideux! presque autant que moi.
Je bois, c'est honteux, presque plus que toi,
Ce n'est plus ce qu'on appelle une vie...
Ah! la femme, fol, fol est qui s'y fie!

Les hommes, bravo! c'est fier et soumis,
On peut s'y fier, voilà des amis!
Nous buvons, mais, vous mesdames, l'ivresse
Vous va moins qu'à nous, — te change en tigresse.

    Moi tout au plus en un simple cochon;
    Quelque idéal sot dans mon cabochon,
    Quelque bêtise en sus, quelque sottise
    En outre, — mais toi, la fainéantise,

    La méchanceté, l'obstination,
    Un peu le vice et beaucoup l'option,
    Pour être plus folle, sur ma parole!
    Que ma folie à moi déjà si folle.

    Ces réflexions me coûtent beaucoup,
    Mais ce soir je suis d'une humeur de loup.
    Excuse, si mon discours va si rogue,
    Mais ce soir je suis d'une humeur de dogue.

. . . .

Bah! buvons pas trop (s'il nous est possible),
Ma bouche est un trou, la tienne est un crible.
Dieu saura bien reconnaître les siens.
Morale: surtout baisons-nous — et viens!

XIII

    Es-tu brune ou blonde?
    Sont-ils noirs ou bleus,
        Tes yeux?
Je n'en sais rien, mais j'aime leur clarté profonde,
Mais j'adore le désordre de tes cheveux.

    Es-tu douce ou dure?
    Est-il sensible ou moqueur,
        Ton cœur?
Je n'en sais rien, mais je rends grâce à la nature
D'avoir fait de ton cœur mon maître et mon vainqueur.

    Fidèle, infidèle?
    Qu'est-ce que ça fait.
        Au fait?
Puisque, toujours disposé à couronner mon zèle
Ta beauté sert de gage à mon plus cher souhait.

XIV

Je ne t'aime pas en toilette
Et je déteste la voilette
Qui t'obscurcit tes yeux, mes cieux,
Et j'abomine la «tournure»
Parodie et caricature,
De tels tiens appas somptueux.

Je suis hostile à toute robe
Qui plus ou moins cache et dérobe
Ces charmes, au fond les meilleurs:
Ta gorge, mon plus cher délice,
Tes épaules et la malice
De tes mollets ensorceleurs.

Fi d'une femme trop bien mise!
Je te veux, ma belle, en chemise,
— Voile aimable, obstacle badin,
Nappe d'autel pour l'alme messe.
Drapeau mignard vaincu sans cesse
Matin et soir, soir et matin.

XV

Chemise de femme, armure *ad hoc*
Pour les chers combats et le gai choc,
Avec, si frais et que blancs et gras,
Sortant tout nus, joyeux, les deux bras,

    Vêtement suprême,
    De mode toujours,
    C'est toi seul que j'aime
    De tous ses atours.

Quand Elle s'en vient devers le lit,
L'orgueil des beaux seins cambrés emplit
Et bombe le linge tout parfumé
Du seul vrai parfum, son corps pâmé.

    Vêtement suprême,
    De mode toujours,
    C'est toi seul que j'aime
    De tous ses atours.

Quand elle entre dans le lit, c'est mieux
Encor: sous ma main le précieux
Trésor de sa croupe frémit dans
Les plis de batiste redondants.

    Vêtement suprême,
    De mode toujours,
    C'est toi seul que j'aime
    De tous ses atours.

Mais lorsqu'elle a pris place à côté
De moi, l'humble serf de sa beauté,
Il est divin et mieux mon bonheur
À bousculer le linge et l'honneur!

Vêtement suprême.
De mode toujours.
C'est toi seul que j'aime
De tous ses atours.

XVI

L'été ne fut pas adorable
Après cet hiver infernal,
Et quel printemps défavorable!
Et l'automne commence mal,
  Bah! nous nous réchauffâmes
  En mêlant nos deux âmes.

La pauvreté, notre compagne
Dont nous nous serions bien passés,
Vainement menait la campagne
Durant tous ces longs mois glacés...
  Nous incaguions l'intruse,
  Son astuce et sa ruse.

Et riches, de baisers sans nombre,
— La seule opulence, crois-moi, —
Que nous fait que le temps soit sombre
S'il fait soleil en moi, chez toi.
  Et que le plaisir rie
  À notre gueuserie?

XVII

Je ne suis plus de ces esprits philosophiques,
Et ce n'est pas de morale que tu te piques
Deux admirables conditions pour l'amour
Tel que nous l'entendrons, c'est-à-dire sans tour
Aucun de bête convenance ou de limites,
Mais chaud, rieur — et zut à tous us hypocrites!

    Aimons gaîment
    Et franchement.

J'ai reconnu que la vertu, quand s'agit d'Elles,
Est duperie et que la plupart d'elles ont
Raison de s'en passer, nous prenant pour modèles:
Si bien qu'il est très bien de faire comme font
Les bonnes bêtes de la terre et les célestes,
N'est-ce pas? prompts moineaux, n'est-ce pas, les cerfs prestes.

    Aimons bien fort
    Jusqu'à la mort.

Pratique mon bon conseil et reste amusante.
S'il se peut, sois-le plus encore et représente
Toi bien que c'est ta loi d'être pour nous charmer
Et la fleur n'est pas plus faite pour se fermer
Que vos cœurs et vos sens, ô nos belles amies...
Tête en l'air, sens au clair, vos «pudeurs» endormies,

    Aimons dûment
    Et verdement.

XVIII

Si tu le veux bien, divine Ignorante,
Je ferai celui qui ne sait plus rien
Que te caresser d'une main errante.
En le geste expert du pire vaurien,

Si tu le veux bien, divine Ignorante.

Soyons scandaleux sans plus nous gêner
Qu'un cerf et sa biche ès bois authentiques.
La honte, envoyons-la se promener.
Même exagérons et, sinon cyniques,

Soyons scandaleux sans plus nous gêner.

Surtout ne parlons pas littérature.
Au diable lecteurs, auteurs, éditeurs
Surtout! Livrons-nous à notre nature
Dans l'oubli charmant de toutes pudeurs,

Et, ô! ne parlons pas littérature!

Jouir et dormir, ce sera, veux-tu?
Notre fonction première et dernière,
Notre seule et notre double vertu,
Conscience unique, unique lumière.

Jouir et dormir, m'amante, veux-tu?

XIX

Ton rire éclaire mon vieux cœur
Comme une lanterne une cave
Où mûrirait tel cru vainqueur:
Aï, Beaune, Sauterne, Grave.

Ton rire éclaire mon vieux cœur.

Ta voix claironne dans mon âme:
Tel un signal d'aller au feu...
... De tes yeux en effet tout flamme
On y va, sacré nom de Dieu!

Ta voix claironne dans mon âme.

Ta manière, ton *meneo*,
Ton chic, ton galbe, ton que sais-je,
Me disent: «Viens çà» *Prodeo*.
(Ô ces souvenirs de collège!)

Ta manière! ton *meneo*!

Ta gorge, tes hanches, ton geste,
Et le reste, odeur et fraîcheur
Et chaleur m'insinuent: reste!
Si j'y reste, en ton lit mangeur!

Ta gorge, tes hanches! ton geste!

XX

Tu crois au marc de café,
 Aux présages, aux grands jeux:
Moi je ne crois qu'en tes grands yeux.

Tu crois aux contes de fées,
 Aux jours néfastes, aux songes,
Moi je ne crois qu'en tes mensonges.

Tu crois en un vague Dieu
 En quelque saint spécial,
En tel Ave contre tel mal.

Je ne crois qu'aux heures bleues
 Et rose que tu m'épanches
Dans la volupté des nuits blanches!

Et si profonde est ma foi
 Envers tout ce que je crois
Que je ne vis plus que pour toi.

XXI

Lorsque tu cherches tes puces,
      C'est très rigolo.
Que de ruses, que d'astuces!
      J'aime ce tableau.
C'est, alliciant en diable
      Et mon cœur en bat
D'un battement préalable
      À quelque autre ébat

Sous la chemise tendue
      Au large, à deux mains
Tes yeux scrutent l'étendue
      Entre tes durs seins.
Toujours tu reviens bredouille,
      D'ailleurs, de ce jeu.
N'importe, il me trouble et brouille,
      Ton sport, et pas peu!

Lasse-toi d'être défaite
      Aussi sottement,
Viens payer une autre fête
      À ton corps charmant
Qu'une chasse infructueuse
      Par monts et par vaux.
Tu seras victorieuse...
      Si je ne prévaux!

XXII

J'ai rêvé de toi cette nuit:
Tu te pâmais en mille poses
Et roucoulais des tas de choses...

Et moi, comme on savoure un fruit,
Je te baisais à bouche pleine
Un peu partout, mont, val ou plaine.

J'étais d'une élasticité,
D'un ressort vraiment admirable:
Tudieu, quelle haleine et quel rable!

Et toi, chère, de ton côté,
Quel rable, quelle haleine, quelle
Élasticité de gazelle...

Au réveil ce fut, dans tes bras,
Mais plus aiguë et plus parfaite,
Exactement la même fête!

XXIII

Je n'ai pas de chance en femme,
Et, depuis mon âge d'homme,
Je ne suis tombé guère, en somme.
Que sur des criardes infâmes.

C'est vrai que je suis criard
Moi-même et d'un révoltant
Caractère tout autant,
Peut-être plus par hasard.

Mes femmes furent légères,
Toi-même tu l'es un peu,
Cet épouvantable aveu
Soit dit entre nous, ma chère.

C'est vrai que je fus coureur.
Peut-être le suis-je encore:
Cet aveu me déshonore.
Parfois je me fais horreur.

Baste: restons tout de même
Amants fervents, puisqu'en somme
Toi, bonne fille et moi, brave homme,
Tu m'aimes, dis, et que je t'aime.

XXIV

Bien qu'elle soit ta meilleure amie,
C'est farce ce que nous la trompons
Jusques à l'excès, sans penser mie
À elle, tant nos instants sont bons,

Nos instants sont bons!

Je fais des comparaisons, de même
Toi cocufiant ton autre amant,
Et je dois dire que ton système
Pour le cocufier est charmant.

Ton us est charmant!

Mon plaisir est d'autant plus coupable
(Et plus exquis, grâce à ton concours)
Qu'elle se montre aussi très capable
Et fort experte aux choses d'amours.

Mais sans ton concours?

Trompons-la bien, car elle nous trompe
Peut-être aussi, tant on est coquins
Et qu'il n'est de pacte qu'on ne rompe.
Trompons-les bien. Nuls remords mesquins!

Soyons bien coquins!

XXV

Je fus mystique et je ne le suis plus
(La femme m'aura repris tout entier),
Non sans garder des respects absolus
Pour l'idéal qu'il fallut renier.

Mais la femme m'a repris tout entier!

J'allais priant le Dieu de mon enfance
(Aujourd'hui c'est toi qui m'as à genoux),
J'étais plein de foi, de blanche espérance.
De charité sainte aux purs feux si doux.

Mais aujourd'hui tu m'as à tes genoux!

La femme, par toi, redevient le maître,
Un maître tout-puissant et tyrannique,
Mais qu'insidieux! feignant de tout permettre
Pour en arriver à tel but satanique...

Ô le temps béni quand j'étais ce mystique!

Odes en Son Honneur (French)

I

Tu fus une grande amoureuse
À ta façon, la seule bonne
Puisqu'elle est tienne et que personne
Plus que toi ne fut malheureuse,
Après la crise de bonheur
Que tu portas avec honneur.

Oui, tu fus comme une héroïne,
Et maintenant tu vis, statue
Toujours belle sur la ruine
D'un espoir qui se perpétue
En dépit du Sort évident,
Mais tu persistes cependant!

Pour cela, je t'aime et t'admire
Encore mieux que je ne t'aime
Peut-être, et ce m'est un suprême
Orgueil d'être meilleur ou pire
Que celui qui fit tout le mal,
D'être à tes pieds tremblant, féal!

Use de moi, je suis ta chose;
Mon amour va, ton humble esclave,
Prêt à tout ce que lui propose
Ta volonté dure et suave,
Prompt à jouir, prompt à souffrir,
Prompt vers tout, hormis pour mourir!

Mourir dans mon corps et mon âme,
Je le veux si c'est ton caprice.
Quand il faudra que je périsse
Tout entier, fais un signe, femme,
Mais que mon amour dût cesser?

Il ne peut que s'éterniser.

Jette un regard de complaisance,
Ô femme forte, ô sainte, ô reine,
Sur ma fatale insuffisance
Sans doute à te faire sereine:
Toujours triste du temps fané,
Du moins, souris au vieux damné.

II

Laisse dire la calomnie
Qui ment, dément, nie et renie
Et la médisance bien pire
Qui ne donne que pour reprendre
Et n'emprunte que pour revendre...
Ah! laisse faire, laisse dire!

Faire et dire lâches et sottes,
Faux gens de bien, feintes mascottes.
Langue d'aspic et de vipère;
Ils font des gestes hypocrites,
Ils clament, forts de leurs mérites,
Un mal de toi qui m'exaspère,

Moi qui t'estime et te vénère
Au-dessus de tout sur la terre,
T'estime et vénère, ma belle,
De l'amour fou que je le voue,
Toi, bonne et sans par trop de moue,
M'admettant au lit, ma fidèle!

Mais toi, méprise ces menées,
Plus haute que tes destinées,
Grand cœur, glorieuse martyre,
Plane au-dessus de tes rancunes
Contre ces d'aucuns et d'aucunes;
Bah! laisse faire et laisse dire!

Bah! fais ce que tu veux, ma belle
Et bonne, — fidèle, infidèle, —
Comme tu fis toute ta vie,
Mais toujours, partout, belle et bonne,
Et ne craignant rien de personne,
Quoi qu'en aient la haine et l'envie.

Et puis tu m'as, si tu m'accordes

Un peu de ces miséricordes
Qui siéient envers un birbe honnête.
Tu m'as, chère, pour te défendre,
Te plaire, si tu veux m'entendre
Et voir, encore que laid et bête.

III

L'écartement des bras m'est cher, presque plus cher
        Que l'écartement autre:
Mer puissante et que belle et que bonne de chair,
        Quel appât est la vôtre!

Ô seins, mon grand orgueil, mon immense bonheur,
        Purs, blancs, joie et caresse,
Volupté pour mes yeux et mes mains et mon cœur
        Qui bat de votre ivresse,

Aisselles, fins cheveux courts qu'ondoie un parfum
        Capiteux où je plonge,
Cou gras comme le miel, ambré comme lui, qu'un
        Dieu fit bien mieux qu'en songe.

Fraîcheur enfin des bras endormis et rêveurs
        Autour de mes épaules,
Palpitantes et si doux d'étreinte à mes ferveurs
        Toutes à leurs grands rôles,

Que je ne sais quoi pleure en moi, peine et plaisir.
        Plaisir fou, chaste peine,
Et que je ne puis mieux assouvir le désir
        De quoi mon âme est pleine

Qu'en des baisers plus langoureux et plus ardents
        Sur le glorieux buste
Non sans un sentiment comme un peu triste dans
        L'extase comme auguste!

Et maintenant vers l'ombre blanche — et noire un peu,
        L'amour il peut détendre
Plus par en bas et plus intime son fier jeu
        Dès lors naïf et tendre!

IV

La sainte, ta patronne, est surtout vénérée
Dans nos pays du Nord et toute la contrée
Dont je suis à demi, la Lorraine et l'Ardenne.
Elle fut courageuse et douce et mourut vierge
Et martyre. Or il faut lui brûler un beau cierge
En ce jour de ta fête et de quelque fredaine
De plus, peut-être, en son honneur, ô ma païenne!

Tu n'es pas vierge, hélas! mais encore martyre
Non pour Dieu, mais qui te plut. (Qu'ont-ils à rire?)
A cause de ton cœur saignant resté sublime.
Courageuse, tu l'es, pauvre chère adorée,
Pour supporter tant de douleur démesurée
Avec cette fierté qui pare une victime,
Avec tout ce pardon joyeux et longanime.

Et douce? Ah oui! malgré ton allure si vive
Et si forte et rude parfois. Douce et naïve
Comme ta voix d'enfant aux notes paysannes.
Douce au pauvre et naïve envers tous et que bonne
Sous un dehors souvent brutal qui vous étonne,
Vous, les gens, mais dont j'ai vite su les arcanes!

Douce et bonne et naïve, âme exquise qui planes
Au-dessus de tout préjugé bête ou féroce,
Au-dessus de l'hypocrisie et du cant rosse
Et du jargon menteur et de l'argot fétide
Dans la région pure où la haine s'ignore,
Où la rancune expire, où l'amour pur arbore
Sur la blancheur des cieux sa bannière candide.
Ô résignation infiniment splendide.

En ce jour de ta fête et malgré nos frivoles
Préoccupations moins coupables que folles
De baisers redoublés pour le cas, et l'antienne
Plus gentille encor qu'excessive des mots lestes,

Recueillons-nous pourtant, pensons aux fins célestes
Afin qu'après ma mort ou, las! après la tienne,
Le survivant pour l'absent prie, ô ma chrétienne!

V

« Quand je cause avec toi paisiblement,
Ce m'est vraiment charmant, tu causes si paisiblement !

Quand je dispute et te fais des reproches,
Tu disputes, c'est drôle, et me fais aussi des reproches.

S'il m'arrive, hélas ! d'un peu te tromper,
misère ! tu cours la ville afin de me tromper.

Et si je suis depuis des temps fidèle,
Tu me restes, durant juste tous ces temps-là, fidèle.

Suis-je heureux, tu te montres plus heureuse
Encore, et je suis plus heureux, d'enfin ! te voir heureuse.

Pleuré-je, tu pleures à mon côté.
Suis-je pressant, tu viens bien gentiment de mon côté.

Quand je me pâme, lors tu te pâmes.
Et je me pâme plus de sentir qu'aussi tu te pâmes.

Ah ! dis quand je mourrai, mourras-tu, toi ? »
Elle : « Comme je t'aimais mieux, je mourrai plus que toi. »

... Et je me réveillai de ce colloque
Hélas ! C'était un rêve (un rêve ou bien quoi ?) ce colloque.

VI

Mais après les merveilles
Qui n'ont pas de pareilles
De l'épaule et du sein,
Faut sur un autre mode
Dresser une belle ode
Au glorieux bassin.

Faut célébrer la blanche
Souplesse de la hanche
Et sa mate largeur,
Dire le ventre opime
Et sa courbe sublime
Vers le sexe mangeur

Que chastement, encore
Que joliment, décore
Et défend juste assez
L'ombre qui sied aux choses
Divines, peu moroses
Rideaux drûment tressés.

Teutatès adorable,
Saturne plus aimable,
Anthropophage cher
Qui veut aux sacrifices
Non le sang des génisses
Mais le lait de ma chair.

Nous chanterons ensuite
L'aine blonde et sa fuite
Ambrée au sein du Saint...
Mais déposons la lyre.
Livrons-nous au délire
Raisonnable et succinct?

Non! fou, braque, orgiaque.

En apache, en canaque
Ivre de tafia :
Nous ne sommes pas l'homme
Pour la docte Sodome
Quand la Femme il y a.

VII

Fifi s'est réveillé. Dès l'aube tu m'as dit
Bonjour en deux baisers, et le pauvre petit
Pépia, puis remit sa tête sous son aile
Et tut pour le moment sa gente ritournelle.
Ici je te rendis pour les tiens un baiser
Multiforme, ubiquiste et qui fut se poser
De la plante des pieds au bout des cheveux sombres
Avec des stations aux lieux d'éclairs et d'ombres,
Un jeu (car tu riais) ridiculement doux,
Et, brusque, entre les tiens je poussai mes genoux,

Tôt redressé sur eux et, penché vers ta bouche,
Fus brutal sans que tu te montrasses farouche,
Car tu remerciais dans un regard mouillé
C'est alors que Fifi, tout à fait réveillé,

Le mignon compagnon! comparable aux bons drilles
Que le bonheur d'autrui ne fait pas envieux,
Salua mon triomphe en des salves de trilles
Que tout son petit cœur semblait lancer aux cieux.

Il sautillait, fiérot, comme un gars qui se cambre,
Acclamant un vainqueur justement renommé,
Et l'aurore éclatant aux carreaux de la chambre
Attestait sans mentir que nous avions aimé.

VIII

Cuisses grosses mais fuselées.
Tendres et fermes par dessous,
Dessus d'un dur qui serait doux,
Musculeuses et potelées,

Cuisses si bonnes tant baisées
Devers leur naissance et par là,
Blanches plus que rose-thé, la
Meilleure part de mes pensées,

Genoux, petites têtes d'anges
Bouffis dans leur juste maigreur,
Mollets bondis qui font fureur
En des bas clairs craignant les fanges.

Pieds dressés pour te hausser jusque
A ma taille pour t'embrasser,
Moi, t'enlever et te placer
Sur le lit, pieds très beaux que busque

La cheville de mol ivoire
Et que parfume leur fraîcheur;
Doigts délicats, frêle rougeur
Doucement fauve au talon, voire

Assez forte peau pour la marche,
Mais quoi! faut-il pas au cher corps
Base solide et soutiens forts,
Au cher corps qui garde mon Arche,

L'arche de crainte et de blandices
Où j'entre, tous torts révolus,
Comme on monterait au ciel. Pieds
Divins, genoux fins, bonnes cuisses!

IX

Tu fus souvent cruelle,
Même injuste parfois,
Mais que fait, ô ma belle,
Puisqu'en toi seule crois

Et puisque suis ta chose.

Que tu me trompes avec Pierre,
Louis, et cœtera punctum,
Je sais, mais, là! n'en ai que faire:
Ne suis que l'humble factotum

De ton humeur gaie ou morose.

S'il arrive que tu me battes,
Soufflettes, égratignes, tu
Es le maître dans nos pénates,
Et moi le cocu, le battu,

Suis content et vois tout en rose.

   Et puis dame j'opine
   Qu'à me voir ainsi si
   Tien, finiras, divine
   Par m'aimoter ainsi

Qu'on s'attache à sa chose.

X

Et maintenant, aux Fesses !
Je veux que tu confesses,
Muse, ces miens trésors
Pour quels — et tu t'y fies —
Je donnerais cent vies
Et, riche, tous mes ors
Avec un tas d'encors.

Mais avant la cantate
Que mes âme et prostate
Et mon sang en arrêt
Vont dire à la louange
De son cher Cul que l'ange,
O déchu ! saluerait,
Puis il l'adorerait,

Posons de lentes lèvres
Sur les délices mièvres
Du dessous des genoux,
Souple papier de Chine,
Fins tendons, ligne fine
Des veines sans nul pouls
Sensible, il est si doux !

Et maintenant, aux Fesses !
Déesses de déesses,
Chair de chair, beau de beau.
Seul beau qui nous pénètre
Avec les seins, peut-être.
D'émoi toujours nouveau,
Pulpe dive, alme peau !

Elles sont presques ovales,
Presque rondes. Opales,
Ambres, roses (très peu)
S'y fondent, s'y confondent

En blanc mat que répondent
Les noirs, roses par jeu,
De la raie au milieu.

Déesses de déesses!
Du repos en liesses,
De la calme gaîté,
De malines fossettes
Ainsi que des risettes,
Quelque perversité
Dans que de majesté...!

Et quand l'heure est sonnée
D'unir ma destinée
A Son Destin fêté,
Je puis aller sans crainte
Et bien tenter l'étreinte
Devers l'autre côté:
Leur concours m'est prêté.

Je me dresse et je presse
Et l'une et l'autre fesse
Dans mes heureuses mains.
Toute leur ardeur donne,
Leur vigueur est la bonne
Pour aider aux hymens
Des soirs aux lendemains...

Ce sont les reins ensuite,
Amples, nerveux qu'invite
L'amour aux seuls élans
Qu'il faille dans ce monde,
C'est le dos gras et monde,
Satin tiède, éclairs blancs.
Ondulements troublants.

Et c'est enfin la nuque
Qu'il faudrait être eunuque

Pour n'avoir de frissons,
La nuque damnatrice,
Folle dominatrice
Aux frisons polissons
Que nous reconnaissons.

Ô nuque proxénète,
Vaguement déshonnête
Et chaste vaguement,
Frisons, joli symbole
Des voiles de l'Idole
De ce temple charmant,
Frisons chers doublement!

XI

Riche ventre qui n'a jamais porté,
Seins opulents qui n'ont pas allaité,
Bras frais et gras, purs de tout soin servile,

Beau cou qui n'a plié que sous le poids
De lents baisers à tous les chers endroits,
Menton où la paresse se profile,

Bouche éclatante et rouge d'où jamais
Rien n'est sorti que propos que j'aimais,
Oiseux et gais — et quel nid de délices!

Nez retroussé quêtant les seuls parfums
De la santé robuste, yeux plus que bruns
Et moins que noirs, indulgemment complices,

Front peu penseur mais pour cela bien mieux,
Longs cheveux noirs dont le grand flot soyeux,
Jusques aux reins lourdement se hasarde,

Croupe superbe éprise de loisir
Sauf aux travaux du suprême plaisir,
Aux gais combats dont c'est l'arrière-garde,

Jambes enfin, vaillantes seulement
Dans le plaisant déduit au bon moment
Serrant mon buste et ballant vers la nue,

Puis, au repos, — cuisses, genoux, mollet, —
Fleurant comme ambre et blanches comme lait
— Tel le pastel d'après ma femme nue.

XII

Mais Sa tête, Sa tête!
Folle, unique tempôte
D'injustice indignée,
De mensonge en furie,
Visions de tuerie
Et de vengeance ignée.

Puis exquise bonace,
Du soleil plein l'espace.
Colombe sur l'abîme,
Toute bonne pensée
Caressée et bercée
Pour un réveil sublime.

Force de la nature
Magnifiquement dure
Et si douce, Sa tête.
Adoré phénomène
De ma Philomène
La tête, seule fête!

Et voyez quelle est belle
Cette tête rebelle
A la littérature
Comme à l'art de la brosse
Et du ciseau féroce,
Voyez, race future!

Car je veux dire aux Anges
Ce plus cher des visages,
Cheveux noirs comme l'ombre
Où passerait une onde
Pure, froide, profonde,
Sous un ciel bas et sombre,

Petit front d'Immortelle

Plissé dans la querelle,
Nez mignard qu'ironise
Un bout clair qui s'envole,
Bouche d'où Sa parole
Part, précise et consise

Mais sorcière sans cesse,
Qui blesse et qui caressa
Mon âme obéissante,
Soumise, adulatrice,
Voix dominatrice,
Voix toute-puissante...!

Et ô sur cette bouche
Plus âpre que farouche,
Plus farouche que tendre,
Plus tendre qu'ordinaire,
Prince au fond débonnaire,
Le Baiser semble attendre,

Et tout cela qu'éclaire
Le regard circulaire
De deux yeux de braise,
Bruns avec de la flamme,
Sournois avec de l'âme
Et du cœur, n'en déplaise

A nos jaloux, ma reine,
Ma noble souveraine
Qui me lient dans tes geôles,
Tête belle et bonne
Et mauvaise — et couronne
Du trône, tes Épaules.

XIII

Nos repas sont charmants encore que modestes,
Grâce à ton art profond d'accommoder les restes
Du rôti d'hier ou de ce récent pot-au-feu
En hachis et ragoûts comme on n'en trouve pas chez Dieu.

Le vin n'a pas ce nom, car à quoi sert la gloire?
Et puisqu'il est tiré, ne faut-il pas le boire?
Pour le pain, comme on n'en a pas toujours mangé,
Qu'il nous semble excellent me semble un fait archijugé.

Le légume est pour presque rien, et le fromage:
Nous en usons en rois dont ce serait l'usage.
Quant aux fruits, leur primeur ça nous est bien égal,
Pourvu qu'il y en ait dans ce festin vraiment frugal.

Mais le triomphe, au moins pour moi, c'est la salade:
Comme elle en prend! sans jamais se sentir malade,
Plus forte en cela que défunt Tragaldabas,
Et j'en bâfre de cœur tant elle est belle en ces ébats,

Et le café, qui pour ma part fort m'indiffère,
Ce qu'elle l'aime, mes bons amis, quelle affaire!
Je m'en amuse et j'en jouis pour elle, vrai!
Et puis je sais si bien que la nuit j'en profiterai.

Je sais si bien que le sommeil fuira sa lèvre
Et ses yeux allumés encor d'un brin de fièvre
Par la goutte de rhum bue en trinquant gaîment
Avec moi, présage gentil d'un choc bien plus charmant.

XIV

Nous sommes bien faits l'un pour l'autre;
Pourtant quand tu me rencontreras
Menant mes derniers embarras
D'homme grave et de bon apôtre,
Ruine encore de chrétien,
Philosophe déjà païen,

Lourd de doctrine et de scrupule,
(Le tout un peu décomposé)
Mais au fond très bien disposé
Pour la popine et la crapule,
En un mot, sot entre les sots
De cette sorte de puceaux,

T'eus quelque mal à la conquête,
— Et par ce mot que j'ai voulu
J'entends ton triomphe absolu, —
Sinon de mon cœur, de ma tête;
Je ne parle pas de mon corps
Vaincu dès les primes abords.

Mais comme nous sympathisâmes
Dès nos esprits mis en rapport
Et dès lors quel parfait accord
Entre ces luronnes, nos deux âmes,
Ces luronnes et nos lurons
D'esprits tout carrés et tout ronds!

Toi simple encor, que compliquée,
Et moi naïf aux cents replis,
Notre expérience des lits
Et noire ignorance marquée
En fait de sentiment subtil,
Tout ce nous rendait que gentil

L'un à l'autre! en dépit, par crises,

De colères bien vite au trot,
D'humeurs noires, roses bientôt,
Et, mon Dieu, d'un tas de sottises
Qu'on réparait, pour t'apaiser
Madame et Monsieur, d'un baiser!

C'est de persévérer, petite!
C'est, chère, de continuer,
Quittes à parfois nous tuer
Pour nous ressusciter ensuite,
C'est de rester à deux, vraiment,
Bon cœur et mauvais garnement.

XV

Quand tu me racontes les frasques
De ta chienne de vie aussi,
Mes pleurs tombent gros, lourds, ainsi
Que des fontaines dans des vasques,
Et mes longs soupirs condolents
Se mêlent à tes récits lents.

Tu me dis tes amours premières :
Fille des champs avec des gars,
Puis fille en ville aux fols écarts
Et les trahisons coutumières
Et mutuelles sans remord
Des deux parts et comme d'accord.

Tout d'un coup un caprice vite
Mûri, par l'us, en passion
Sauvage, tel l'humble scion
Grandissant en palme subite
Qu'agiterait dans quelque vert
Paysage un vent du désert.

Fidèle, toi, l'autre, infidèle.
Toi douloureuse, lâche, enfin
Furieuse, soûle du vin
Du vice, essorant d'un coup d'aile
Ton cœur comme un aigle blessé,
Mais sans pouvoir fuir le passé...

Je t'écoute, et ma pitié toute.
Toute mon admiration,
Une indicible affection,
Sinon celle d'un pur amour
Te vont de moi par quelle route
Qui souffrirait, chère, à son tour,

Qui souffrira, j'en ai la crainte.

Qui souffre déjà, tu le sais,
Toi parfois mauvaise à l'excès.
Charmante aussi comme une sainte
Envers ce moi, bon vieil amant,
Le dernier, hein, probablement?

XVI

Je ne suis pas jaloux de ton passé, chérie,
Et même je t'en aime et t'en admire mieux.
Il montre ton grand coeur et la gloire inflétrie
D'un amour tendre et fort autant qu'impétueux.

Car tu n'eus peur ni de la mort ni de la vie,
Et, jusqu'à cet automne fier répercuté
Vers les jours orageux de ta prime beauté,
Ton beau sanglot, honneur sublime, t'a suivie.

Ton beau sanglot que ton beau rire condolait
Comme un frère plus mâle, et ces deux bons génies
T'ont sacrée à mes yeux de vertus infinies
Dont mon amour à moi, tout fier, se prévalait

Et se targue pour t'adorer au sens mystique:
Consolations, voeux, respects, en même temps
Qu'humbles caresses et qu'hommages ex-votants
De ma chair à ce corps vaillant, temple héroïque

Où tant de passions comme en un Panthéon,
Rancoeurs, pardons, fureurs et la sainte luxure
Tinrent leur culte, respectant la forme pure
Et le galbe puissant profanés par Phaon.

Pense à Phaon pour l'oublier dans mon étreinte
Plus douce et plus fidèle, amant d'après-midi,
D'extrême après-midi, mais non pas attiédi,
Que me voici, tout plein d'extases et de crainte.

Va, je t'aime... mieux que l'autre: il faut l'oublier.
Toi: souris-moi du moins entre deux confidences,
Amazone blessée ès belles imprudences
Qui se réveille au sein d'un vieux brave écuyer.

XVII

« Tu m'ostines ! » — « Et je t'emmène
A la campagne. » Ainsi parlaient
Deux amoureux dont s'éperlaient
Plus d'un encor propos amène.

Je crains fort que ces amoureux
N'aient été nous l'autre semaine
Nous répondant, Tyrcis, Climène,
Hélas ! en mots trop savoureux.

Mais puisqu'il en est temps encore,
Puisqu'il en est encore temps,
Ne soyons donc plus mécontents,
Au contraire, et que s'édulcore

Notre courroux, pourtant grondant
Un petit peu, mais pour la forme,
En un orage horrible, énorme,
De gros baisers se répondant.

Ô ma dure et bonne compagne,
Assez, dis, de malentendus,
Et si tu veux — car je le dus —
Or, je t'emmène à la campagne.

XVIII

Ô toi triomphante sur deux
«Rivales» (pour dire en haut style).
Tu fus ironique, — elles... feues —
Et n'employas d'effort subtil
Que juste assez pour que tu fus —
Ses encor mieux, grâce à cet us

Qu'as de me plaire sans complaire
Plus qu'il ne faut à mes caprices.
Or je te viens jouer un air
Tout parfumé d'ambre et d'iris,
Bien qu'ayant en horreur triplice
Tout parfum hostile ou complice,

Sauf la seule odeur de toi, frais
Et chaud effluve, vent de mer
Et vent, sous le soleil, de prées
Non sans quelque saveur amère
Pour saler et poivrer ainsi
Qu'il est urgent, mon cœur transi.

Mon cœur, mais non pas ma bravoure
En fait d'amour! Tu ressuscite-
Rais un défunt, le bandant pour
Le déduit dont Vénus dit: Sit!
Oui, mon cœur encore il pantèle
Du combat court, mais de peur telle!

Peur de te perdre si le sort
Des armes eût trahi tes coups.
Peur encor de toi, peur encore
De tant de boudes et de moues.
Quant aux deux autres, ô là là!
Guère n'y pensais, t'étais là.

Iris, ambre, ainsi j'annonçai

— Ma mémoire est bonne — ces vers
A ta victoire fière et gaie
Sur tes rivales somnifères.
Mais que n'ont-ils le don si cher,
Si pur? Fleurer comme ta chair!

XIX

Ils me disent que tu me trompes.
D'abord, qu'est-ce que ça leur fait?
Chère frivole, que tu rompes
Un serment que tu n'as pas fait?

Ils me disent que t'es méchante
Envers moi, — moi, qui suis si bon!
Toi méchante! Qu'un autre chante
Ce refrain très loin d'être bon

Méchante, toi qui toujours m'offres
Un sourire amusant toujours,
Toi, ma reine, qui de tes coffres
Me puise des trésors toujours.

Ils me disent et croient bien dire,
Ô toi que tu ne m'aimes pas?
Que m'importe, j'ai ton sourire,
Et puis tu ne m'aimerais pas?

Tu ne m'aimes? Et la grâce
Et la force de ta beauté.
Tu me les donnes, grande et grasse
Et voluptueuse beauté.

Tu ne m'aimes pas? Et quand même
Ce serait vrai, qu'est-ce que fait?
«Si tu ne m'aimes pas, je t'aime.»
— Mais tu m'aimes, dis, par le fait.

Other Books by the Publisher

Fanchette's Pretty Little Foot
by Restif de La Bretonne,
translated by Richard Robinson

Je M'Accuse...
by Léon Bloy,
translated by Richard Robinson

My Hospitals & My Prisons
by Paul Verlaine,
translated by Richard Robinson

Salvation Through the Jews
by Léon Bloy,
translated by Richard Robinson

Words of a Demolitions Contractor
by Léon Bloy,
translated by Richard Robinson

Cellulely
by Paul Verlaine,
translated by Richard Robinson

Ecclesiastical Laurels
by Jacques Rochette de la Morlière,
translated by Richard Robinson

Flowers of Bitumen
by Émile Goudeau
translated by Richard Robinson

www.ingramcontent.com/pod-product-compliance
Lightning Source LLC
Chambersburg PA
CBHW060615080526
44585CB00013B/835